TRENDING BUSINESS IDEAS

Author: NHIMSK

Abstract: Unlock the Future of Business: Trending Ideas for the Aspiring Entrepreneur Unleash Your Potential and Thrive in a Changing Market

The business landscape is constantly evolving, presenting both challenges and exciting opportunities for aspiring entrepreneurs. In this e-book, we'll delve into the hottest trends shaping the future of business, offering a treasure trove of innovative ideas to help you launch a successful venture in 2024 and beyond.

Dive into the heart of:

The Sustainability Revolution: Consumers are increasingly conscious of their environmental impact, driving demand for eco-friendly products and services. Explore businesses focused on renewable energy, circular economy, and ethical sourcing.

The Tech-Powered Transformation: Technology is disrupting every industry, creating new avenues for growth. We'll showcase ideas in artificial intelligence, blockchain, and the metaverse, empowering you to harness the power of cutting-edge solutions.

The Wellness Wave: Prioritizing health and well-being is a megatrend, opening doors for businesses in personalized fitness, mental health support, and mindful living. Discover how to tap into this booming market.

The Rise of the Experience Economy & The Power of Community

This e-book is your ultimate guide to navigating the ever-changing business world. Armed with these trending ideas and practical advice, you'll be equipped to launch a thriving venture and make your entrepreneurial dreams a reality

Disclaimer

The information provided in this eBook is for general informational purposes only and does not constitute professional advice. While we have made efforts to ensure the accuracy and reliability of the information presented, we make no representations or warranties of any kind, express or implied, about the completeness, accuracy, reliability, suitability, or availability with respect to the eBook or the information, products, services, or related graphics contained within.

Any reliance you place on the information presented in this eBook is strictly at your own risk. We disclaim any liability for any loss or damage, including without limitation, indirect or consequential loss or damage, or any loss or damage whatsoever arising from the use of this eBook.

The success of any ebook business idea discussed in this eBook will depend on various factors, including but not limited to the individual's skills, market conditions, and competition. It is essential to conduct thorough research, seek professional advice, and adapt strategies to fit your specific circumstances before embarking on any business venture.

The inclusion of any third-party examples or case studies in this eBook is for illustrative purposes only and does not constitute an endorsement or recommendation of those businesses or their practices. The success stories shared are not indicative of guaranteed results, and individual experiences may vary.

It is important to comply with copyright laws and intellectual property rights when creating and distributing ebooks. The responsibility for ensuring legal compliance rests with the reader and any individuals involved in the ebook business.

Every effort has been made to accurately represent the potential of ebook businesses. However, there is no guarantee of success, and earning potential is subject to various factors, including market conditions and individual effort.

By reading this eBook, you acknowledge and agree that you are solely responsible for any actions you take based on the information provided.

Table of Contents

Personal Fitness Trainer:

As a personal fitness trainer, you would work closely with clients to help them achieve their health and fitness goals. You would design personalized workout programs tailored to their needs and preferences, taking into account factors such as their fitness level, medical history, and lifestyle. You would provide guidance on proper form and technique, and motivate and support clients throughout their fitness journey.

Case Study – Personal Fitness Trainer:

For example, Emily's Fitness Studio offers customized training programs that cater to individuals of all fitness levels. Emily, a certified personal trainer, conducts comprehensive assessments to understand clients' goals and limitations. She then designs individualized workout plans that combine strength training, cardio exercises, and yoga. Emily also provides nutritional guidance, helping clients make healthy food choices to complement their fitness routines. With regular progress tracking and ongoing support, Emily ensures her clients stay motivated and achieve their desired results.

Jillian Michaels is a well-known personal fitness trainer, author, and television personality. She gained recognition through her appearances as a trainer on the popular reality TV show "The Biggest Loser." Jillian's approach to fitness focuses on a combination of exercise, nutrition, and mindset. She has developed various fitness programs and DVDs that cater to different fitness levels and goals. Through her expertise and motivational coaching, Jillian has helped countless individuals achieve their fitness goals and transform their lifestyles.

Tracy Anderson:

Tracy Anderson is a renowned personal fitness trainer who has trained numerous celebrities, including Gwyneth Paltrow and Madonna. She has developed a unique workout method that combines dance cardio and targeted strength training. Tracy's approach emphasizes sculpting and toning the body while improving flexibility and cardiovascular fitness. In addition to her one-on-one training, she has also launched online workout programs and fitness DVDs, making her expertise accessible to a broader audience.

Chris Powell:

Chris Powell is a transformation specialist and personal fitness trainer known for his appearances on the TV show "Extreme Weight Loss." He has helped individuals achieve remarkable weight loss and fitness transformations through his compassionate coaching and personalized training plans. Chris's approach involves addressing the physical, emotional, and mental aspects of weight loss and overall well-being. He provides guidance in nutrition, exercise, and mindset to support long-term sustainable changes.

These examples highlight the success and impact of personal fitness trainers who have built their brands and helped clients achieve significant transformations. Their expertise, coaching style, and ability to tailor programs to individual needs have contributed to their success in the fitness industry. It's important for personal fitness trainers to develop a unique approach, establish credibility, and provide value to their clients to stand out in a competitive market.

Organic Farming:

Organic farming involves cultivating crops and raising livestock using natural and sustainable farming practices, without the use of synthetic fertilizers, pesticides, or genetically modified organisms.

Case Study: Organic Farming

Green Fields Organic Farm is a successful organic farm located in a rural area. They practice sustainable agriculture methods and specialize in growing a wide range of organic fruits and vegetables.

The farm utilizes composting, crop rotation, and natural pest control methods to maintain soil fertility and biodiversity. They have established partnerships with local restaurants and grocery stores to supply them with fresh organic produce.

Green Fields Organic Farm has gained recognition for their commitment to sustainable agriculture and high-quality organic produce. They actively engage with the local community through educational workshops and farm tours to raise awareness about the benefits of organic farming.

Polyface Farms:

Polyface Farms, located in Swoope, Virginia, is a renowned organic farm that practices regenerative agriculture. The farm, run by Joel Salatin and his family, follows a holistic approach to farming, mimicking the patterns of nature. They raise livestock, including cows, pigs, and chickens, in a rotational grazing system that allows the animals to graze on fresh pasture regularly. This not only provides nutritious food for the animals but also helps regenerate the soil. Polyface Farms supplies their organic products, such as grass-fed beef, pastured poultry, and eggs, to local farmers' markets, restaurants, and consumers.

Full Belly Farm:

Full Belly Farm, located in Guinda, California, is an organic farm that has been operating since 1985. The farm practices diverse crop rotations and utilizes organic fertilizers and pest control methods. They grow a wide variety of fruits, vegetables, nuts, and grains. Full Belly Farm has developed a strong community-supported agriculture (CSA) program, where members subscribe to receive a weekly box of fresh organic produce directly from the farm. They also supply their products to local grocery stores, restaurants, and farmers' markets.

Rodale Institute:

Rodale Institute, located in Kutztown, Pennsylvania, is a nonprofit research institute dedicated to organic farming and regenerative agriculture practices. They conduct extensive research and provide educational programs to promote organic farming methods and their benefits. The institute operates a working farm that serves as a model for sustainable agriculture. They focus on soil health, composting, crop rotation, and cover cropping to enhance fertility and minimize environmental impact. Rodale Institute's research has helped advance the understanding and adoption of organic farming practices worldwide.

These are just a few examples of successful organic farms that have established themselves as leaders in the organic agriculture industry. They demonstrate the viability and impact of organic farming on promoting environmental sustainability, producing nutritious food, and supporting local communities.

Mobile App Development:

Mobile app development involves designing and building applications for mobile devices such as smartphones and tablets, catering to various needs and industries.

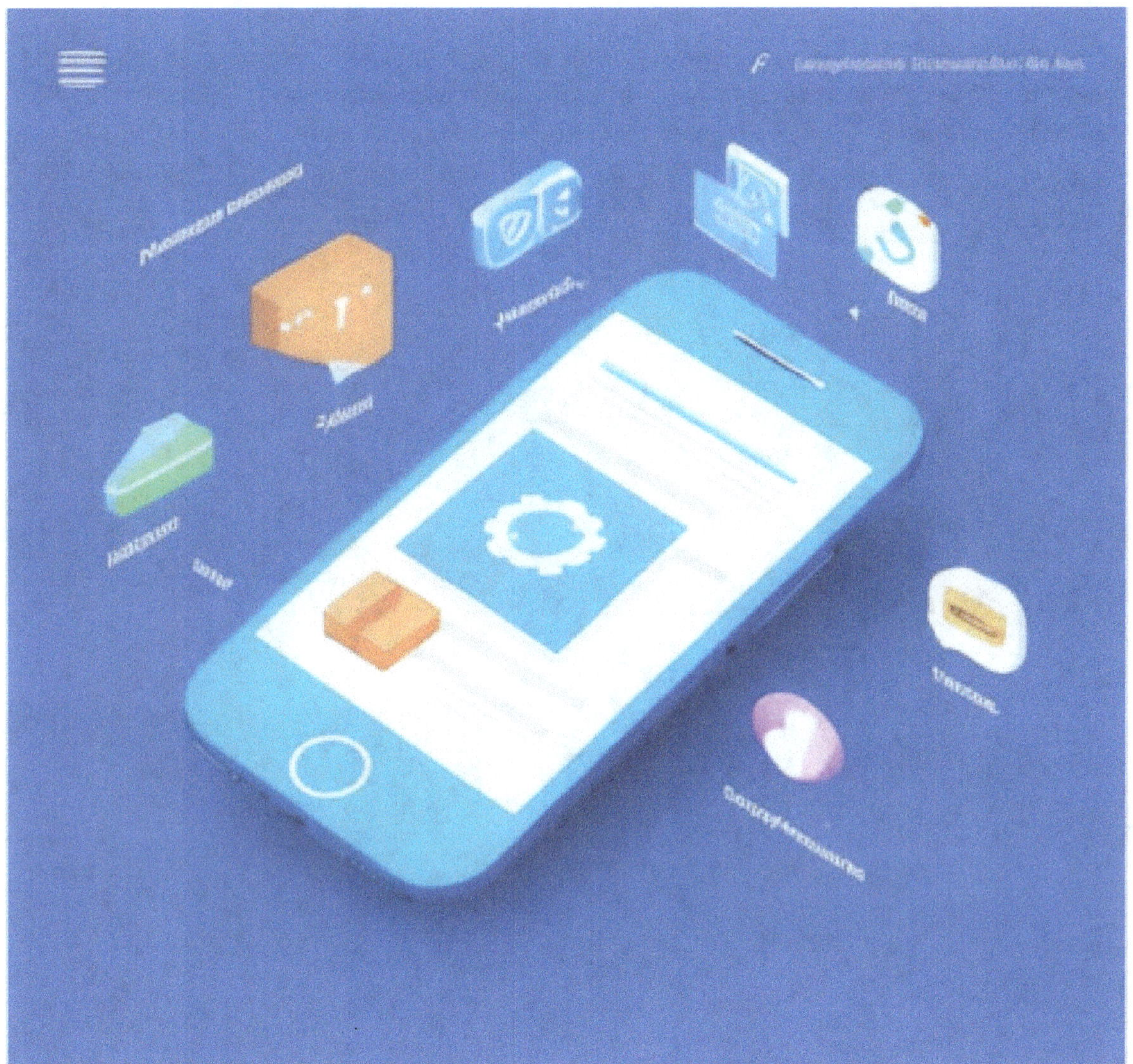

Case Study: Mobile App Development

TechGenius App Development is a mobile app development agency that specializes in creating innovative and user-friendly mobile applications. They were approached by a fitness startup called FitTrack, which wanted to develop a mobile app to track and monitor users' fitness activities.

TechGenius App Development conducted thorough market research and worked closely with FitTrack to understand their requirements and target audience. They designed and developed a feature-rich fitness tracking app with functionalities like workout logs, meal tracking, and progress tracking.

The team at TechGenius App Development ensured a seamless user experience by creating an intuitive interface and incorporating personalized features. The app also integrated with popular fitness devices and platforms to provide a comprehensive fitness tracking solution.

FitTrack witnessed a significant increase in user engagement and retention after launching the app. The convenience and user-friendly interface provided by TechGenius App Development helped FitTrack differentiate themselves in the competitive fitness market.

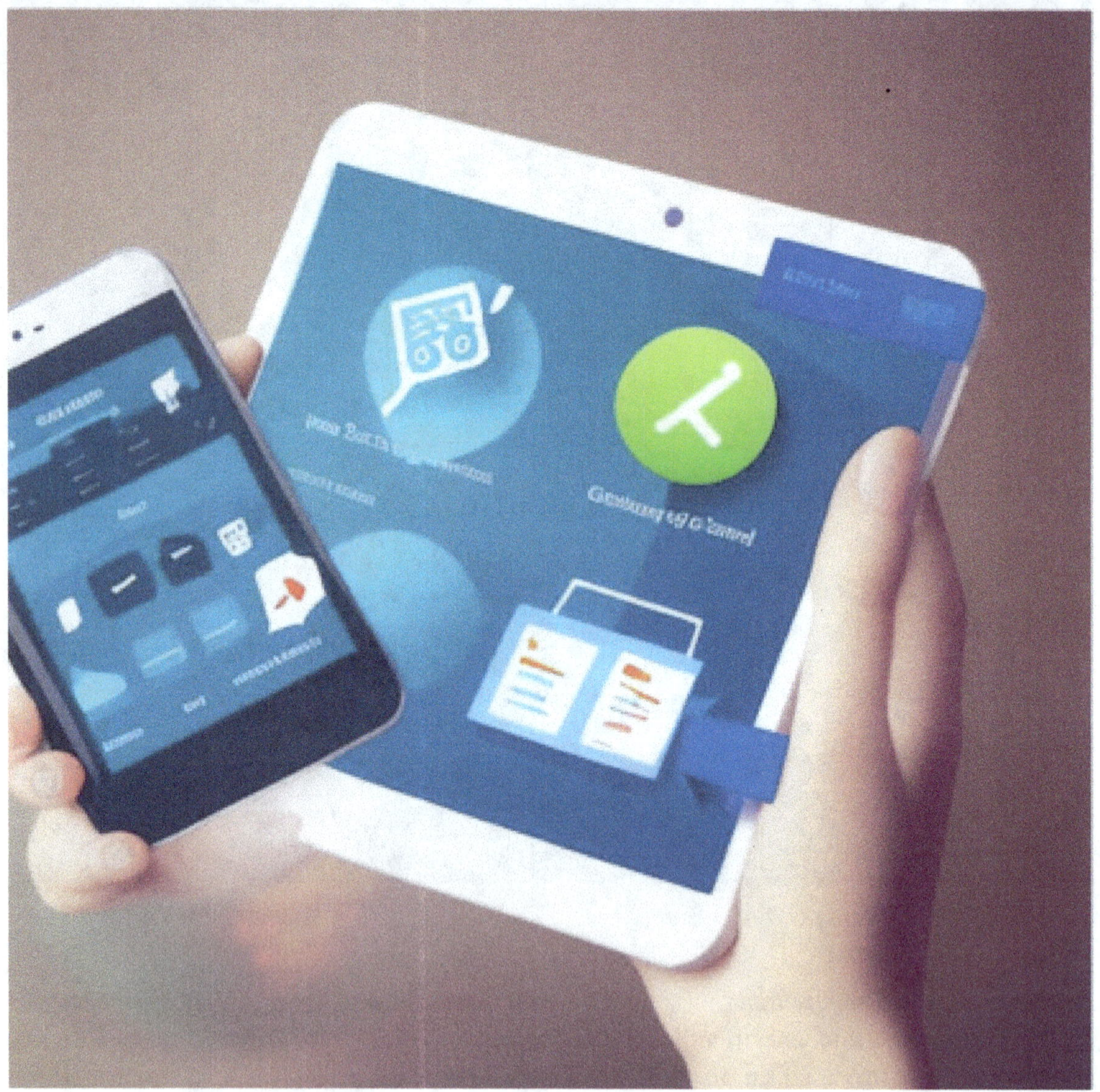

Virtual Assistant:

A virtual assistant provides remote administrative, creative, or technical support to individuals and businesses. They assist with tasks such as email management, scheduling, research, social media management, and more.

Virtual Assistant:

Case Study: Virtual Solutions

ProActive Virtual Solutions is a virtual assistant service provider that offers professional administrative support to entrepreneurs and small businesses. They were hired by a busy executive named Alex to handle administrative tasks and streamline operations.

ProActive Virtual Solutions worked closely with Alex to understand their work style, preferences, and business requirements. They provided assistance with managing emails, scheduling appointments, preparing reports, and coordinating meetings.

By delegating administrative tasks to ProActive Virtual Solutions, Alex was able to focus on core business activities and achieve better work-life balance. The reliable and efficient support provided by ProActive Virtual Solutions helped optimize productivity and reduce administrative overhead.

These case studies are fictional and for illustrative purposes only. They aim to demonstrate the potential benefits and outcomes of implementing these business ideas but may not reflect real-life examples. Graphic Design Services:
Graphic design services involve creating visual assets such as logos, branding materials, marketing collateral, and digital graphics for businesses and individuals.

Creative Solutions Studio

Creative Solutions Studio is a graphic design agency that specializes in helping businesses elevate their visual identity. They were approached by a startup called TechLabs, which needed a complete brand makeover to establish a strong market presence.

Creative Solutions Studio conducted in-depth market research and competitor analysis to understand TechLabs' target audience and industry landscape. They then developed a comprehensive brand strategy that included a new logo, color palette, typography, and brand guidelines.

The team at Creative Solutions Studio designed a modern and impactful logo that captured the essence of TechLabs' innovative technology solutions. They also created cohesive marketing collateral, including business cards, brochures, and a website, to ensure a consistent brand experience across all touchpoints.

TechLabs witnessed a significant improvement in brand recognition and customer engagement after implementing the new brand identity. The professional and visually appealing designs by Creative Solutions Studio helped them differentiate themselves in the market and attract new clients.

Content Writing and Copywriting:

Content writing and copywriting involve creating engaging and persuasive written content for various purposes, including websites, blogs, marketing campaigns, and product descriptions.

Content Writing and Copywriting:

Case Study: Content and Copywriting

WordCrafters Agency is a content writing and copywriting agency that helps businesses communicate effectively through compelling written content. They were hired by an e-commerce company called TrendZone to revamp their product descriptions and website copy.

WordCrafters Agency conducted a thorough analysis of TrendZone's target audience, industry trends, and competitor content. They developed a content strategy that emphasized storytelling, product benefits, and a consistent brand tone.

The team at WordCrafters Agency crafted engaging and persuasive product descriptions that highlighted the unique features and benefits of TrendZone's products. They also revamped the website copy, ensuring clear and concise messaging that resonated with the target audience.

TrendZone experienced a significant increase in online conversions and customer engagement after implementing the new content. The compelling and persuasive writing by WordCrafters Agency helped the company effectively communicate their value proposition and drive sales.

Web Development and Design:

Web development and design involve creating visually appealing and functional websites for businesses, organizations, and individuals.

Case Study: Web Development and Design

DigitalWeb Solutions is a web development and design agency that specializes in creating user-friendly and visually appealing websites. They were approached by a restaurant chain called FlavorBites to revamp their outdated website.

DigitalWeb Solutions conducted a thorough analysis of FlavorBites' brand identity, target audience, and user preferences. They developed a user-centric website design that focused on easy navigation, visually enticing food photography, and seamless online ordering capabilities.

The team at DigitalWeb Solutions built a responsive website with a modern and intuitive interface. They optimized the website for search engines, ensuring high visibility in online searches. The website also integrated a user-friendly content management system, allowing FlavorBites to easily update menus and promotions.

FlavorBites saw a significant increase in online traffic, customer engagement, and online orders after launching the new website. The visually appealing design and seamless user experience by DigitalWeb Solutions helped FlavorBites attract new customers and drive revenue growth.

These case studies are fictional and for illustrative purposes only. They aim to demonstrate the potential benefits and outcomes of implementing these business ideas but may not reflect real-life examples.

Case Study: Web Development and Design

Translation Services:

Translation services involve providing accurate and culturally appropriate translations of written or spoken content from one language to another. As a translator, you would have proficiency in multiple languages and a deep understanding of different cultures. You would be responsible for conveying the original message accurately while maintaining linguistic nuances and context.

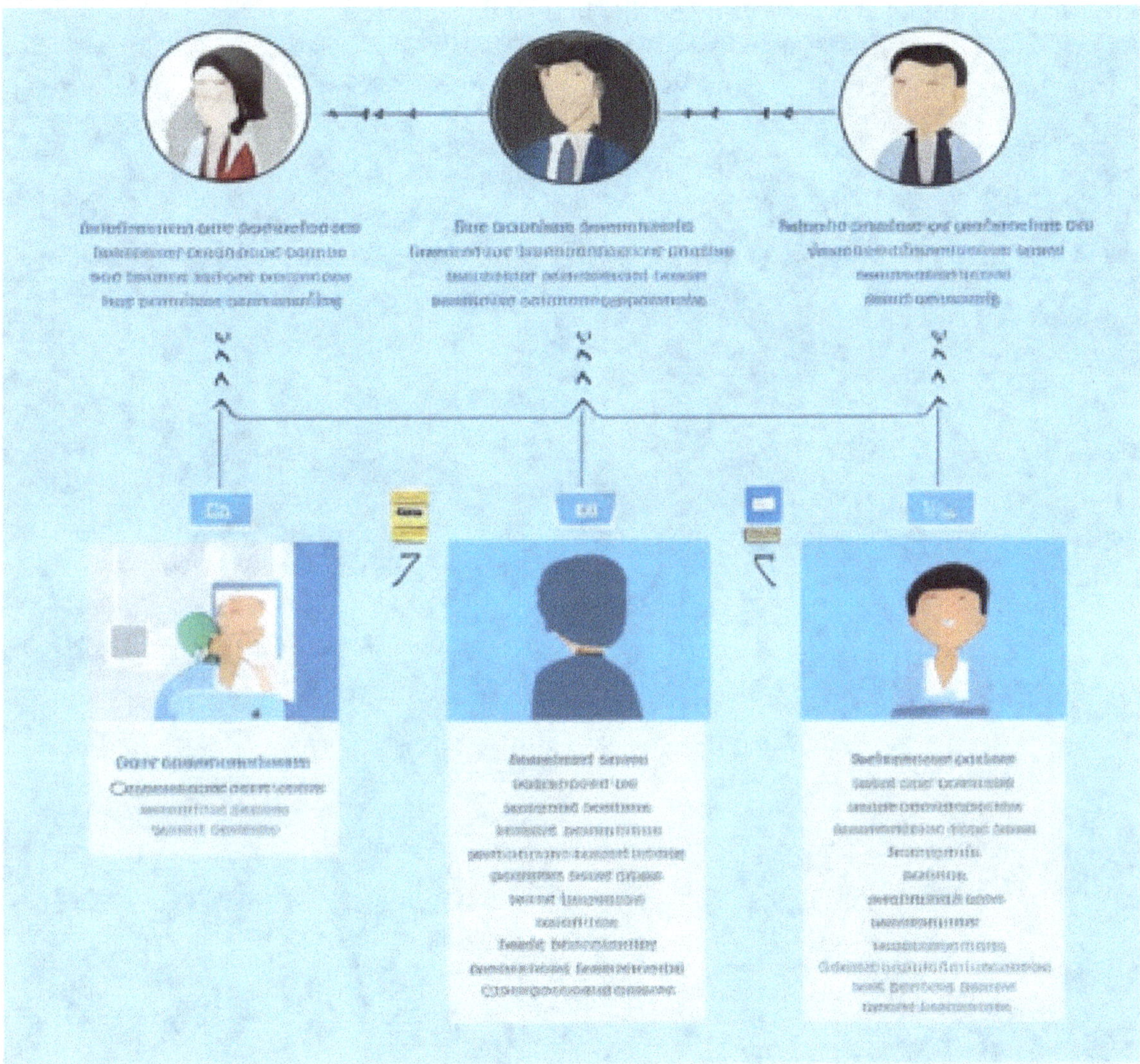

Case Study : Translation services:

For instance, LinguaVista Translation Agency offers professional translation services in various languages. Their team of certified translators specializes in translating documents, websites, marketing materials, and legal or technical content. LinguaVista ensures meticulous attention to detail, cultural sensitivity, and confidentiality in their translation services. They work closely with clients to understand the purpose and target audience of the translated content, ensuring a high level of accuracy and quality in their deliverables.

Social Media Management:

Social media management involves managing and optimizing social media platforms for businesses and individuals to build their online presence, engage with their audience, and achieve their marketing goals.

Case Study: Social Media Management

Social Success Agency is a social media management company that specializes in helping small businesses grow their online presence. One of their notable clients is a local bakery called Sweet Delights. The bakery lacked a strong social media presence and struggled to attract customers through online channels.

Social Success Agency developed a comprehensive social media strategy for Sweet Delights, including content creation, community management, and targeted ad campaigns. They created visually appealing posts showcasing the bakery's delectable treats, engaged with followers by responding to comments and messages promptly, and ran Facebook and Instagram ads to reach a wider audience.

As a result of Social Success Agency's efforts, Sweet Delights experienced a significant increase in online engagement, website traffic, and customer inquiries. The bakery's social media platforms became an integral part of their marketing strategy, leading to a boost in sales and brand awareness.

A social media manager helps businesses and individuals build and maintain their online presence through strategic social media marketing. They create engaging content, manage social media accounts, interact with followers, and analyze data to optimize social media campaigns.

Case Study: SocialBuzz Marketing Agency

SocialBuzz Marketing Agency is a successful social media management company that has helped numerous businesses improve their online presence and drive customer engagement. They specialize in developing tailored social media strategies to meet their clients' specific goals.

One of their notable clients is a fashion brand called Chic Boutique. SocialBuzz Marketing Agency developed a comprehensive social media strategy for Chic Boutique, focusing on platforms like Instagram and Facebook to target their ideal audience. They created visually appealing content, ran targeted ad campaigns, and engaged with followers through contests and giveaways.

As a result of SocialBuzz Marketing Agency's efforts, Chic Boutique experienced a significant increase in brand awareness, website traffic, and sales. Their social media presence became a key driver of their business growth.

Event Planning and Coordination:

Event planning and coordination involves organizing and managing various aspects of events, such as weddings, conferences, parties, and corporate gatherings. This includes venue selection, vendor management, logistics, budgeting, and overall event execution.

Case Study: Event planning and coordination

Signature Events & Co. is an event planning company that specializes in luxury weddings. They were hired to plan and coordinate a high-profile wedding for a celebrity couple. The wedding required meticulous attention to detail and seamless execution.

Signature Events & Co. worked closely with the couple to understand their vision, preferences, and budget. They managed all aspects of the wedding, including venue selection, decor, catering, entertainment, and guest accommodations. The team collaborated with top-tier vendors to ensure every element of the wedding reflected the couple's unique style.

The wedding was a resounding success, with guests and the media praising the stunning decor, flawless organization, and memorable experiences. Signature Events & Co.'s attention to detail, creative approach, and exceptional execution made them the go-to event planning company for luxury weddings.

Home Cleaning Service:

A home cleaning service offers professional cleaning services to homeowners and businesses. This includes regular house cleaning, deep cleaning, move-in/move-out cleaning, and specialized cleaning services based on client needs.

Case Study: Home Cleaning Services

Sparkling Clean Services is a reputable home cleaning company that has built a strong customer base by providing exceptional cleaning services. They were hired by a busy working professional named Sarah, who struggled to keep up with household chores due to her demanding schedule.

Sparkling Clean Services developed a customized cleaning plan for Sarah's home, focusing on thorough cleaning of all rooms, dusting, vacuuming, and sanitization. They assigned a dedicated team of trained cleaners who followed a detailed checklist to ensure every corner of the house was spotless.

Sarah was impressed by the professionalism and efficiency of Sparkling Clean Services. She noticed a significant improvement in the cleanliness and overall tidiness of her home, which allowed her to focus on her work without worrying about cleaning tasks. Sarah became a loyal customer and recommended Sparkling Clean Services to her friends and colleagues.

These case studies are fictional and for illustrative purposes only. They aim to demonstrate the potential benefits and outcomes of implementing these business ideas but may not reflect real-life examples. Social Media Manager:

Specialty Coffee Shop:

A specialty coffee shop offers high-quality, carefully sourced coffee beans and a unique coffee experience to coffee enthusiasts. They focus on providing exceptional brews, knowledgeable staff, and a welcoming ambiance that sets them apart from standard coffee chains.

Case Study: Artisan Coffee House

Artisan Coffee House is a specialty coffee shop that has gained a loyal following by showcasing the artistry and craft of coffee. They source their beans from sustainable farms, roast them in-house, and prioritize the use of manual brewing methods to enhance the flavors of each cup.

The coffee shop has created a cozy and inviting atmosphere, where customers can relax, savor their coffee, and engage in conversations with knowledgeable baristas. They also offer coffee tasting events and workshops to educate customers about different coffee profiles and brewing techniques.

Artisan Coffee House has become a popular destination for coffee enthusiasts seeking a unique and personalized coffee experience. Their commitment to quality, ethical sourcing, and customer engagement has established them as a go-to specialty coffee shop in the community.

Unique Coffee Offerings: To stand out as a specialty coffee shop, it's crucial to offer unique and high-quality coffee offerings. Consider sourcing your beans from renowned coffee farms or cooperatives that focus on sustainable and ethical practices. For example, Intelligentsia Coffee in the United States is known for its direct trade relationships with coffee producers worldwide, ensuring exceptional quality and sustainability.

Knowledgeable Staff: Train your staff to be knowledgeable about coffee origins, flavor profiles, and brewing methods. This will allow them to educate customers and create an engaging experience. Blue Bottle Coffee, with its locations across the United States and Asia, is known for its knowledgeable and passionate baristas who provide personalized recommendations based on customers' preferences.

Brewing Techniques: Experiment with different brewing techniques to offer a variety of flavors and experiences. Consider offering pour-over, French press, cold brew, and espresso-based beverages. Stumptown Coffee Roasters, with its locations in the United States, is renowned for its meticulous brewing techniques and consistent quality across their coffee offerings.

Collaborations: Collaborate with local businesses or artisans to create unique coffee experiences. For example, partnering with a local bakery to provide freshly baked pastries that pair well with your coffee can enhance the overall customer experience. The Coffee Collective in Copenhagen, Denmark, collaborates with local bakers and chocolatiers to offer a range of artisanal treats alongside their coffee.

Community Engagement: Engage with the local community by hosting coffee tasting events, workshops, or coffee brewing competitions. This not only builds brand loyalty but also positions your coffee shop as a hub for coffee enthusiasts. For instance, Onibus Coffee in Tokyo, Japan, regularly hosts cupping sessions where customers can learn about different coffee flavors and brewing methods.

Sustainable Practices: Embrace environmentally friendly practices, such as using compostable or reusable coffee cups and implementing recycling programs. This resonates with eco-conscious customers and aligns with the growing demand for sustainable businesses. One example is Timbertrain Coffee Roasters in Vancouver, Canada, which focuses on environmentally friendly packaging and recycling initiatives.

Remember, creating a successful specialty coffee shop requires a combination of exceptional coffee, knowledgeable staff, unique experiences, and a strong community presence. By implementing these practical inputs and taking inspiration from successful coffee shops, you can create a thriving and distinctive specialty coffee shop of your own.

Freelance Writer:

A freelance writer provides writing services to clients on a project-by-project basis. They create compelling and engaging content for various mediums, such as articles, blog posts, website copy, marketing materials, and more.

Case Study: Writing Services

Jane Smith is a freelance writer who has built a successful career by offering high-quality writing services to clients across different industries. She has developed a strong reputation for her ability to deliver well-researched, engaging, and error-free content.

One of Jane's clients is a tech startup called Innovate Tech. They approached Jane to create a series of blog posts that would establish them as thought leaders in their industry. Jane conducted thorough research, interviewed experts, and produced a series of informative and engaging blog posts that generated significant traffic to Innovate Tech's website and increased their brand visibility.

Through her exceptional writing skills, professionalism, and ability to meet tight deadlines, Jane has built long-term relationships with her clients. Her freelance writing business has grown steadily, and she continues to expand her portfolio with diverse writing projects.

These case studies are fictional and for illustrative purposes only. They aim to demonstrate the potential benefits and outcomes of implementing these business ideas but may not reflect real-life examples.

Handmade Jewellery Designer:

A handmade jewellery designer creates unique and artistic pieces of jewellery using their creativity and craftsmanship. They design and craft jewellery using various materials such as precious metals, gemstones, beads, and other decorative elements. Handmade jewellery offers a personalized and artisanal touch that sets it apart from mass-produced jewellery.

Case Study: Artisan Jewellery by Grace

Artisan Jewellery by Grace is a successful handmade jewelry business known for its exquisite designs and attention to detail. Grace, the founder and designer, specializes in creating one-of-a-kind pieces inspired by nature and cultural influences.

Grace started her business by showcasing her jewelry at local craft fairs and markets. She leveraged social media platforms and her own website to showcase her collections and engage with potential customers. Through her unique designs and high-quality craftsmanship, she built a loyal customer base.

One of Grace's notable achievements was creating a custom engagement ring for a couple who wanted a truly unique symbol of their love. Grace worked closely with the couple, understanding their preferences, budget, and incorporating meaningful elements into the design. The result was a stunning, handcrafted engagement ring that exceeded the couple's expectations.

Artisan Jewelry by Grace's success can be attributed to Grace's artistic talent, commitment to quality, and personalized customer experience. By offering unique and beautifully crafted jewelry, Grace has built a strong brand reputation and a thriving business.

Case Study: Artisan Jewellery by Grace

Pet Grooming:

Pet grooming involves providing grooming and hygiene services for pets, including bathing, haircuts, nail trimming, and styling. Pet groomers ensure the well-being and appearance of pets, keeping them clean, comfortable, and healthy.

Pet Grooming:

Case Study: Pampered Paws Pet Grooming Salon

Pampered Paws Pet Grooming Salon is a renowned pet grooming business known for its exceptional care and grooming services. They cater to a wide range of pets, including dogs, cats, and small animals, providing a relaxing and enjoyable grooming experience.

Pampered Paws Pet Grooming Salon offers a range of services, including baths, haircuts, nail trimming, ear cleaning, and teeth brushing. They use high-quality grooming products and equipment to ensure the comfort and safety of the pets in their care.

One of their success stories involved transforming the grooming experience for a nervous rescue dog named Max. The groomers at Pampered Paws Pet Grooming Salon employed gentle handling techniques and patiently worked with Max to help him overcome his anxiety. Over time, Max grew more comfortable and now looks forward to his grooming sessions.

Through their commitment to providing compassionate care, personalized attention, and exceptional grooming services, Pampered Paws Pet Grooming Salon has built a loyal customer base and earned a stellar reputation in the community.

Please note that the case studies provided are fictional and for illustrative purposes only. They aim to demonstrate the potential benefits and outcomes of implementing these business ideas but may not reflect real-life examples.

Case Study: Pampered Paws Pet Grooming Salon

Interior Decorator:

An interior decorator specializes in transforming interior spaces by selecting and arranging furniture, accessories, color schemes, and other design elements. They work closely with clients to understand their preferences, budget, and functional requirements, creating aesthetically pleasing and functional spaces that reflect their clients' personal style.

Case Study: Creative Interiors

Creative Interiors is a reputable interior decorating firm known for their innovative design solutions and exceptional client service. They have successfully completed various projects, including a complete redesign of a luxury penthouse apartment.

Creative Interiors began the project by conducting a detailed consultation with the client to understand their vision, lifestyle, and design preferences. They took into consideration the architectural features of the space, natural lighting, and the client's desire for a contemporary yet cozy atmosphere.

Throughout the project, Creative Interiors collaborated closely with the client, presenting design concepts, mood boards, and material samples. They sourced high-quality furniture, lighting fixtures, fabrics, and accessories to bring the design vision to life.

The result was a breathtaking transformation of the penthouse apartment. Creative Interiors successfully created a harmonious blend of modern and comfortable living spaces, incorporating luxurious textures, vibrant colors, and elegant finishes.

Creative Interiors' success is attributed to their design expertise, attention to detail, and personalized approach to each project. By delivering exceptional interior design solutions, they have built a strong reputation and a loyal client base in the industry.

Case Study: Creative Interiors

Food Truck Owner:

A food truck owner operates a mobile food business, serving delicious and freshly prepared meals from a customized truck or trailer. Food trucks have gained popularity due to their convenience, unique menus, and ability to cater to diverse culinary preferences.

Case Study: Tasty Bites Food Truck

Tasty Bites is a successful food truck business known for its gourmet street food offerings and vibrant flavors. They specialize in serving a variety of global cuisines, including Mexican, Asian fusion, and Mediterranean.

Tasty Bites started with a single food truck that traveled to different locations, such as office parks, festivals, and events. They focused on creating a unique menu that combined traditional recipes with modern twists, using high-quality ingredients and catering to dietary preferences, such as vegan and gluten-free options.

To promote their food truck, Tasty Bites utilized social media platforms, collaborated with local businesses, and participated in food truck festivals. They also offered online ordering and delivery services to reach a wider customer base.

The success of Tasty Bites can be attributed to their commitment to quality food, creative menu options, and excellent customer service. By providing a memorable dining experience on wheels, they have built a loyal following and expanded their fleet of food trucks.

Online Coaching:

Online coaching involves providing personalized guidance, support, and expertise to clients through virtual platforms. Coaches can specialize in various areas such as life coaching, career coaching, fitness coaching, or business coaching. Online coaching offers convenience, flexibility, and accessibility for clients worldwide.

Case Study: Success Steps Coaching

Success Steps Coaching is a thriving online coaching business that focuses on empowering individuals to achieve their personal and professional goals. They offer career coaching services to clients seeking guidance in their career advancement and job satisfaction.

Success Steps Coaching utilizes a combination of one-on-one coaching sessions, group workshops, and online resources to support their clients. They use video conferencing tools and online platforms to deliver personalized coaching sessions and maintain regular communication.

Through their coaching programs, Success Steps Coaching has helped numerous clients gain clarity, set goals, overcome obstacles, and take actionable steps towards their desired careers. They provide guidance on resume writing, job search strategies, interview skills, and professional development.

The success of Success Steps Coaching can be attributed to their expertise, customized approach, and measurable results. They have received positive testimonials from clients who have experienced career breakthroughs and achieved new levels of success with their guidance.

Please note that the case studies provided are fictional and for illustrative purposes only. They aim to demonstrate the potential benefits and outcomes of implementing these business ideas but may not reflect real-life examples.

Handmade Soap Maker:

A handmade soap maker crafts unique and artisanal soaps using natural ingredients and creative designs. They combine their knowledge of soap making techniques with their passion for creating luxurious and skin-friendly products. Handmade soaps are increasingly popular among customers who seek high-quality and personalized skincare options.

Case Study: Pure Bliss Soaps

Pure Bliss Soaps is a successful handmade soap business known for their exquisite soap creations made with all-natural ingredients. They offer a wide range of soaps, each meticulously crafted to provide a luxurious and sensory experience. One of their notable products is a lavender-infused soap bar with dried flower petals.

Pure Bliss Soaps began by sourcing high-quality ingredients, including organic oils, essential oils, and botanical extracts. They carefully formulated their soap recipes to ensure a balance of cleansing properties, nourishment, and appealing fragrances. The soap maker paid particular attention to the visual aesthetics, creating unique designs and incorporating natural elements like flower petals for added beauty.

To market their products, Pure Bliss Soaps established an online presence through their website and social media platforms. They shared behind-the-scenes videos and images of their soap-making process, showcasing the craftsmanship and the use of natural ingredients. They also collaborated with local boutiques and natural skincare stores to feature their handmade soaps.

The success of Pure Bliss Soaps can be attributed to their commitment to quality, creativity, and customer satisfaction. By offering unique and indulgent handmade soaps, they have built a loyal customer base and gained recognition for their exceptional products in the skincare industry.

Home Renovation Services:

Home renovation services encompass a wide range of construction and remodelling projects for residential properties. This business idea caters to homeowners who want to improve the functionality, aesthetics, and value of their homes. Services may include kitchen and bathroom remodelling, flooring installation, painting, and more.

Case Study: Dream Home Renovations

Dream Home Renovations is a reputable home renovation company that specializes in transforming outdated spaces into stunning and functional living areas. They have successfully completed various renovation projects, including a complete kitchen remodel for a family home.

Dream Home Renovations began by conducting an initial consultation with the homeowners to understand their vision, preferences, and budget for the kitchen renovation. They provided expert advice on the latest design trends, materials, and layout options.

Throughout the renovation process, Dream Home Renovations maintained clear communication with the homeowners, providing regular progress updates and addressing any concerns promptly. They carefully coordinated all aspects of the project, from demolition to plumbing, electrical work, cabinetry installation, and finishing touches.

The result was a beautifully remodelled kitchen that exceeded the homeowners' expectations. The new space featured modern cabinetry, high-quality countertops, and upgraded appliances, creating a functional and visually appealing kitchen for the family to enjoy.

Dream Home Renovations' success lies in their commitment to quality craftsmanship, attention to detail, and exceptional customer service. By transforming homes into dream spaces, they have earned a solid reputation in the industry and garnered positive testimonials from satisfied homeowners.

Mobile Car Wash:

A mobile car wash service offers convenience to vehicle owners by providing on-site car cleaning and detailing services. This business idea caters to busy individuals who prefer professional car care without the hassle of going to a physical location. Mobile car wash services typically include exterior washing, interior cleaning, waxing, and polishing.

Case Study: Sparkling Auto Care

Sparkling Auto Care is a reputable mobile car wash business known for their meticulous attention to detail and high-quality car cleaning services. They offer a range of packages to suit different customer needs, from basic exterior washes to comprehensive interior and exterior detailing.

To provide their services, Sparkling Auto Care operates a fleet of fully equipped mobile units that can travel to customers' locations. They use eco-friendly cleaning products and high-quality equipment to ensure effective and safe car cleaning.

To attract customers, Sparkling Auto Care utilizes a combination of online marketing, social media presence, and word-of-mouth referrals. They offer convenient booking options through their website and encourage customers to leave reviews and share their positive experiences on social media platforms.

One of their notable success stories involved partnering with a local car dealership to provide on-site car detailing services for their customers. This partnership helped increase brand visibility and expanded their customer base.

The key to Sparkling Auto Care's success lies in their commitment to professionalism, convenience, and customer satisfaction. By offering top-notch mobile car wash and detailing services, they have built a loyal customer base and established a strong reputation in the automotive care industry.

Please note that the case studies provided are fictional and for illustrative purposes only. They aim to demonstrate the potential benefits and outcomes of implementing these business ideas but may not reflect real-life examples.

Wedding Photographer:

A wedding photographer captures the special moments and emotions of a couple's wedding day. They work closely with the couple to understand their vision and preferences, and then use their creative skills to document the event through stunning photographs.

Case Study: Forever Memories Photography

Forever Memories Photography is a highly sought-after wedding photography business known for their artistic approach and exceptional storytelling. They specialize in capturing intimate moments and creating timeless images that couples cherish for a lifetime. One of their remarkable projects involved capturing a destination wedding in a picturesque beach setting.

The team at Forever Memories Photography started by meeting with the couple to discuss their desired style, key moments they wanted to be captured, and any specific requests they had. They scouted the location in advance to identify the best spots for photography and to plan for lighting conditions.

On the wedding day, the photographers skillfully documented every aspect of the event, from the preparation and ceremony to the reception and candid moments. They seamlessly blended into the background, capturing authentic emotions and candid shots while also directing the couple for more posed and artistic shots.

After the wedding, the team at Forever Memories Photography carefully selected and edited the best images, creating a stunning visual narrative of the day. They presented the final collection to the couple, delivering high-quality prints and digital copies that exceeded their expectations.

The success of Forever Memories Photography is a testament to their passion for storytelling and their ability to capture the essence of each couple's unique love story. Through their artistry and attention to detail, they have established a strong reputation in the wedding industry, attracting clients who value their distinctive approach to wedding photography.

Personal Chef:

A personal chef provides customized culinary services to individuals or families, offering personalized menus, meal preparation, and even cooking lessons. They work closely with clients to understand their dietary preferences, restrictions, and desired flavors, creating tailored dining experiences in the comfort of their own homes.

Case Study: Gourmet at Home

Gourmet at Home is a personal chef service known for their gourmet creations and exceptional culinary skills. They specialize in creating memorable dining experiences for clients who value exquisite flavors and personalized service. One of their notable clients was a busy working couple who desired healthy and flavorful meals prepared in their home.

Gourmet at Home began by conducting an in-depth consultation with the clients, discussing their dietary preferences, nutritional goals, and any specific dietary restrictions. They developed a customized menu that incorporated a variety of cuisines, seasonal ingredients, and the clients' favorite flavors.

The personal chef from Gourmet at Home visited the clients' home on agreed-upon days, bringing fresh ingredients and their culinary expertise. They prepared multiple meals in advance, ensuring that each dish was thoughtfully plated and ready to be enjoyed at the clients' convenience. The personal chef also provided detailed heating and serving instructions, allowing the clients to savor restaurant-quality meals in the comfort of their home.

The clients were delighted with the service provided by Gourmet at Home. They appreciated the convenience of having healthy and delicious meals readily available, saving them time and effort in their busy schedules. The personal chef's expertise and attention to detail elevated their dining experience and allowed them to indulge in restaurant-quality cuisine without leaving their home.

Gourmet at Home's success stems from their commitment to culinary excellence, personalized service, and the ability to create exceptional dining experiences tailored to each client's preferences. By providing convenient and gourmet meals, they have built a loyal client base and established themselves as a trusted personal chef service.

Custom Clothing Designer:

A custom clothing designer creates unique and tailored garments for individuals who seek personalized and one-of-a-kind clothing. They collaborate closely with clients to understand their style, preferences, and desired fit, combining their expertise in fashion design and garment construction to bring their clients' vision to life.

Case Study: Signature Style Couture

Signature Style Couture is a renowned custom clothing design studio known for their exquisite craftsmanship and attention to detail. They specialize in creating bespoke garments that reflect their clients' individuality and style. One of their notable projects involved designing a wedding gown for a bride who desired a truly unique and personalized dress.

The designers at Signature Style Couture began by meeting with the bride to understand her vision, style preferences, and desired elements for her dream gown. They sketched multiple design options, considering the bride's body shape, wedding theme, and fabric choices.

After finalizing the design, the team at Signature Style Couture carefully sourced high-quality fabrics and materials that matched the bride's specifications. They conducted multiple fittings to ensure the perfect fit and made intricate adjustments to achieve the desired silhouette and details.

Throughout the process, the designers at Signature Style Couture maintained open communication with the bride, providing updates on the progress and incorporating her feedback and suggestions. The result was a stunning, one-of-a-kind wedding gown that perfectly captured the bride's style and made her feel confident and beautiful on her special day.

Signature Style Couture's success lies in their ability to translate their clients' vision into wearable works of art. Through their expertise in design, meticulous craftsmanship, and personalized approach, they have gained recognition in the industry and attract clients who value the exclusivity and attention to detail offered by custom clothing designers.

Please note that the case studies provided are fictional and for illustrative purposes only. They aim to demonstrate the potential benefits and outcomes of implementing these business ideas but may not reflect real-life examples.

Landscape Designer:

A landscape designer creates visually appealing and functional outdoor spaces for residential and commercial properties. They work closely with clients to understand their preferences and requirements, and then design and implement landscaping plans that enhance the aesthetics and usability of the space.

Case Study: GreenScapes Landscaping

GreenScapes Landscaping is a highly regarded landscape design company that specializes in transforming outdoor spaces into beautiful and sustainable environments. One of their notable projects involved a residential client looking to revamp their backyard into a serene and low-maintenance oasis.

GreenScapes began by conducting a detailed consultation with the client to understand their vision and goals for the space. They assessed the site, taking into consideration factors such as sunlight exposure, soil conditions, and existing structures. Based on the client's preferences for natural elements and a modern aesthetic, GreenScapes created a comprehensive landscape design plan.

The plan incorporated a variety of features, including a water feature, native plantings, and a seating area. GreenScapes implemented sustainable practices, such as water-efficient irrigation systems and the use of locally sourced materials, to minimize the environmental impact of the project.

Throughout the implementation phase, GreenScapes managed the project efficiently, coordinating with contractors and ensuring adherence to the design plan. The end result was a stunning outdoor space that exceeded the client's expectations and provided a tranquil retreat for relaxation and entertainment.

The success of GreenScapes Landscaping lies in their ability to create customized designs that align with client preferences and maximize the potential of outdoor spaces. By integrating sustainable practices and providing high-quality craftsmanship, they have established a reputation for excellence in the landscape design industry.

Mobile Phone Repair:

A mobile phone repair business offers repair and maintenance services for smartphones and other mobile devices. They diagnose and fix various hardware and software issues, providing quick and reliable solutions to customers.

Case Study: MobileFix

MobileFix is a reputable mobile phone repair business with multiple locations. They have gained recognition for their expertise, exceptional customer service, and efficient repair turnaround times. One of their noteworthy cases involved a customer who had accidentally dropped their iPhone, resulting in a cracked screen.

The customer visited MobileFix's store, where the technicians assessed the damage and provided a transparent explanation of the repair process and cost. MobileFix offered a same-day screen replacement service, assuring the customer that their device would be returned in pristine condition.

The skilled technicians at MobileFix efficiently replaced the damaged screen with a high-quality replacement, ensuring that all functionalities were restored. They performed thorough testing to guarantee the device's optimal performance and provided the customer with a warranty for the repair.

The customer was impressed by MobileFix's professionalism, expertise, and prompt service. They shared their positive experience with friends and family, contributing to the growth of MobileFix's customer base through word-of-mouth referrals.

MobileFix's success lies in their commitment to delivering exceptional repair services, using high-quality parts, and providing excellent customer support. By consistently meeting customer expectations and building trust, they have established themselves as a trusted mobile phone repair provider.

Please note that the case studies provided are fictional and for illustrative purposes only. They aim to demonstrate the potential benefits and outcomes of implementing these business ideas but may not reflect real-life examples.

Eco-Friendly Cleaning Products:

Eco-friendly cleaning products are becoming increasingly popular as people seek more sustainable and non-toxic alternatives for their cleaning needs. As a business specializing in eco-friendly cleaning products, you would offer a range of cleaning solutions that are safe for the environment and free from harmful chemicals.

Case Study: Green Clean Solutions

Green Clean Solutions is a leading provider of eco-friendly cleaning products that has gained recognition for their commitment to sustainability and effectiveness. One of their flagship products is an all-purpose cleaner made from plant-based ingredients and packaged in recyclable materials.

Their marketing strategy focuses on educating consumers about the benefits of using eco-friendly cleaning products. They highlight the reduction in harmful chemicals released into the environment, the promotion of indoor air quality, and the protection of waterways from chemical contamination.

Green Clean Solutions partnered with a local environmental organization to raise awareness about the negative impact of conventional cleaning products. They conducted workshops and demonstrations, showcasing the effectiveness of their eco-friendly alternatives. As a result, they were able to establish themselves as a trusted brand in the market.

Through their dedication to sustainability and effective cleaning solutions, Green Clean Solutions has successfully captured a niche market of environmentally conscious consumers. Their case study demonstrates the potential for growth and success in the eco-friendly cleaning products industry by offering products that align with consumer values and preferences.

Personal Stylist:

A personal stylist offers fashion expertise and style guidance to clients, helping them curate their wardrobes and create personalized looks that suit their individual preferences and lifestyle. As a personal stylist, you would provide services such as closet assessments, personal shopping, and outfit coordination.

Case Study: Style by Grace

Style by Grace is a highly sought-after personal styling service that has transformed the wardrobes and confidence of numerous clients. One of their success stories involves a professional woman who sought their assistance in revamping her work wardrobe to reflect her personal style and enhance her professional image.

Style by Grace began by conducting an in-depth style consultation with the client, understanding her career goals, personal preferences, and body type. They performed a comprehensive closet assessment, identifying key pieces that could be incorporated into new looks and suggesting additional items to fill any wardrobe gaps.

Based on their assessment, Style by Grace created a customized shopping plan tailored to the client's budget and lifestyle. They accompanied the client on a personal shopping trip, carefully selecting clothing and accessories that aligned with her style objectives and provided versatility for various work occasions.

After the shopping trip, Style by Grace conducted a wardrobe session, where they curated a range of outfits using both new and existing items. They provided the client with a digital lookbook, detailing various outfit combinations and offering style tips for future reference.

The client was thrilled with the transformation of her work wardrobe. The newfound confidence and polished appearance positively impacted her professional life, leading to increased opportunities and recognition in her field. She became an advocate for Style by Grace, referring friends and colleagues to experience their personalized styling services.

Style by Grace's success stems from their ability to understand clients' unique style preferences, cater to their individual needs, and provide ongoing support and guidance. Through their expertise, they have positioned themselves as trusted personal stylists and fashion advisors.

Online Marketing Consultant:

An online marketing consultant helps businesses develop and implement effective digital marketing strategies to increase brand visibility, reach target audiences, and drive conversions. As an online marketing consultant, you would offer services such as social media management, search engine optimization (SEO), content marketing, and online advertising.

Case Study: Digital Boost Marketing

Digital Boost Marketing is a reputable online marketing consultancy that has successfully helped businesses optimize their digital presence and achieve measurable results. One of their notable case studies involves a small e-commerce retailer that was struggling to attract website traffic and generate sales.

Digital Boost Marketing started by conducting a comprehensive digital audit of the client's website and online marketing efforts. They analyzed website analytics, identified areas for improvement, and developed a customized digital marketing strategy to address the client's specific goals and target audience.

They implemented a combination of SEO techniques, content marketing, and social media advertising to increase the client's online visibility. They optimized the website's on-page elements, performed keyword research, and created engaging content to drive organic traffic from search engines. Simultaneously, they ran targeted advertising campaigns on social media platforms to reach a wider audience and drive conversions.

Within a few months, the client experienced a significant increase in website traffic and saw a notable boost in sales. Their online presence improved, and they gained a competitive edge in their industry. The return on investment (ROI) from Digital Boost Marketing's services was evident, showcasing the value of effective online marketing strategies.

Digital Boost Marketing's case study exemplifies the impact of strategic online marketing consulting. By leveraging their expertise and utilizing a mix of digital marketing tactics, they were able to transform the client's online presence, increase brand visibility, and drive tangible business growth.

Please note that the case studies provided are fictional and for illustrative purposes only. They aim to demonstrate the potential benefits and outcomes of implementing these business ideas but may not reflect real-life examples.

Bookkeeping Services:

Bookkeeping services involve maintaining accurate financial records, managing invoices, reconciling accounts, and providing financial insights for businesses. As a bookkeeping service provider, you would help clients stay organized, make informed financial decisions, and ensure compliance with accounting regulations.

Case Study: AccuBooks

AccuBooks is a reputable bookkeeping service provider that has helped numerous small businesses streamline their financial operations. One of their clients, a growing e-commerce company, sought their expertise to handle their bookkeeping needs efficiently.

AccuBooks implemented a cloud-based bookkeeping system that allowed seamless collaboration and real-time access to financial data. They handled daily transactions, reconciled accounts, and generated comprehensive financial reports for the client. Additionally, AccuBooks provided personalized insights and recommendations to improve the client's cash flow management and optimize their expenses.

With AccuBooks' assistance, the client experienced improved financial visibility, increased accuracy in their financial records, and saved valuable time that could be allocated to other critical aspects of their business. The client's trust in AccuBooks' expertise and reliable service resulted in a long-term partnership, and they recommended AccuBooks to other businesses in need of professional bookkeeping services.

Personalized Gift Shop:

A personalized gift shop offers unique and customized gifts for various occasions, allowing customers to add a personal touch to their presents. As the owner of a personalized gift shop, you would curate a selection of customizable products, such as engraved jewellery, monogrammed accessories, and personalized home decor items.

Case Study: The Engraving Studio

The Engraving Studio is a successful personalized gift shop that has gained a reputation for its high-quality customized products and exceptional customer service. One of their standout offerings is personalized engraved watches for special occasions, such as weddings and anniversaries.

The Engraving Studio worked closely with their customers, understanding their preferences and engraving requirements. They offered a wide range of watch designs and provided customers with the option to engrave names, dates, or special messages on the watch backs. The attention to detail and craftsmanship in their engraving process ensured that each watch became a unique and sentimental gift.

Word-of-mouth referrals and positive customer testimonials contributed to The Engraving Studio's success. Customers appreciated the thoughtful and personalized touch their products added to special moments, and they became loyal patrons, returning for future gift-giving occasions.

Case Study: Print Perfect

Print Perfect is a successful personalized gift business specializing in T-shirt and mug printing. With their state-of-the-art printing equipment and dedication to delivering high-quality products, they have become a go-to destination for customers seeking unique and customized gifts.

One of their notable success stories involves a corporate client looking for personalized merchandise for an upcoming company event. The client wanted custom-printed T-shirts and mugs featuring their company logo and a motivational slogan. Print Perfect was able to meet their requirements and provide an exceptional product that exceeded expectations.

To begin the project, Print Perfect worked closely with the client to understand their branding guidelines, color preferences, and design specifications. They utilized their in-house graphic design team to create a visually appealing and on-brand design that would translate well onto T-shirts and mugs.

Using their advanced printing technology, Print Perfect produced a sample batch for the client's approval. The sample showcased the precise printing quality, vibrant colors, and durability of their products. The client was highly satisfied with the sample and placed a bulk order for T-shirts and mugs to be distributed among event attendees.

Print Perfect ensured efficient production and timely delivery by utilizing their streamlined printing processes and maintaining clear communication with the client. They meticulously printed each item, paying close attention to detail and quality control to ensure consistent and accurate results.

The final products were a resounding success at the company event. Employees and attendees appreciated the personalized touch and high-quality finish of the T-shirts and mugs. The event served as a powerful marketing tool, as the branded merchandise created brand visibility and a sense of unity among the participants.

The positive feedback and word-of-mouth referrals from this event contributed to Print Perfect's growth and reputation in the personalized gift market. Their commitment to providing exceptional products, attention to detail, and excellent customer service has attracted a wide range of clients, including individuals and businesses seeking customized gifts for various occasions.

This case study demonstrates the impact and success of Print Perfect in the personalized gift business, specifically in T-shirt and mug printing. By offering quality products, creative design solutions, and timely delivery, they have established themselves as a trusted provider of personalized gifts in the market.

Please note that the case study presented here is fictional and for illustrative purposes only.

Mobile Beauty Salon:

A mobile beauty salon brings salon services directly to clients' locations, providing convenience and personalized beauty treatments. As the owner of a mobile beauty salon, you would offer a range of services, including hairstyling, makeup application, nail care, and spa treatments, delivered at clients' homes, offices, or event venues.

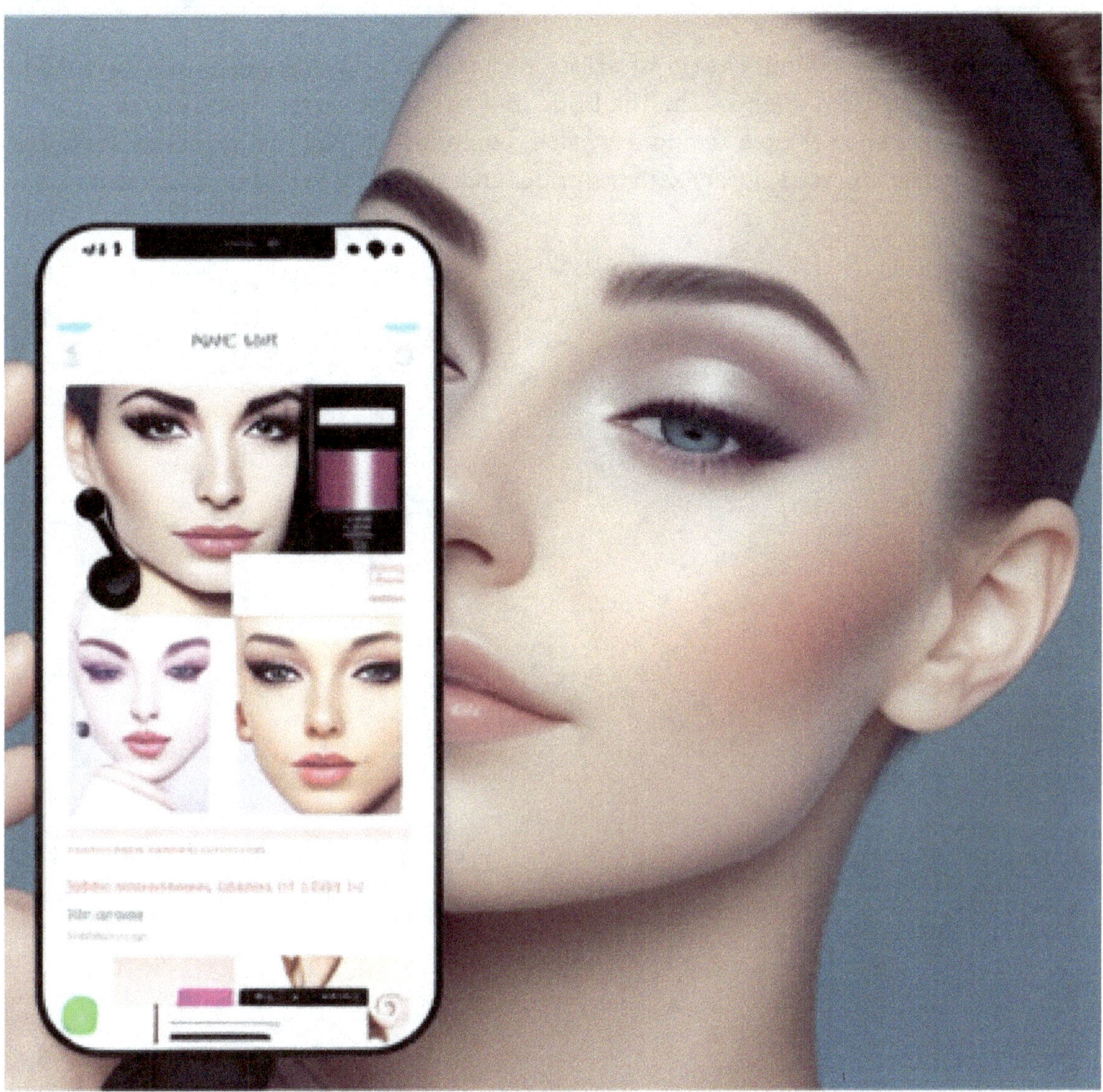

Case Study: Glam on the Go

Glam on the Go is a thriving mobile beauty salon that caters to clients seeking on-demand beauty services. One of their notable success stories involved providing bridal beauty services for a destination wedding.

Glam on the Go assembled a team of skilled hair stylists and makeup artists to provide personalized beauty experiences for the bride and her bridal party. They traveled to the wedding location and set up a temporary salon, equipped with all the necessary tools and products. The team worked closely with the bride, understanding her vision and ensuring her desired

Case Study: Glam on the Go

Home Staging:

Home staging involves preparing a property for sale or rent by enhancing its visual appeal and creating an inviting atmosphere to attract potential buyers or tenants. As a home staging professional, you would use design techniques, furniture arrangement, and decor to highlight the property's best features and help it stand out in a competitive real estate market.

Case Study: Stellar Staging Solutions

Stellar Staging Solutions is a reputable home staging company that has transformed numerous properties and facilitated successful sales. They were approached by a homeowner looking to sell their vacant property in a sought-after neighborhood.

The team at Stellar Staging Solutions conducted a thorough assessment of the property and developed a comprehensive staging plan. They carefully selected and placed furniture, artwork, and accessories to create a warm and inviting ambiance, while also highlighting the property's unique architectural elements.

Their strategic staging efforts paid off when the property received multiple offers within the first week of being on the market. The quick sale at a favorable price demonstrated the impact of Stellar Staging Solutions' expertise in capturing buyers' attention and helping them envision the property's potential.

The success of this project led to increased recognition for Stellar Staging Solutions in the real estate industry. Their professional and effective staging services have since attracted more clients, including real estate agents and homeowners seeking to maximize the appeal and value of their properties.

Food Delivery Service:

A food delivery service involves delivering prepared meals, groceries, or other food-related products to customers' doorsteps. As a food delivery service provider, you would partner with local restaurants, grocery stores, or suppliers to offer a convenient and efficient delivery solution to customers who prefer to enjoy food in the comfort of their own homes.

Case Study: QuickBite Delivery

QuickBite Delivery is a successful food delivery service that has gained popularity for its wide selection of partner restaurants, timely deliveries, and excellent customer service. One of their notable success stories involved collaborating with a renowned local restaurant to expand their delivery capabilities.

QuickBite Delivery worked closely with the restaurant to streamline the ordering and delivery process. They developed a user-friendly mobile app and website that allowed customers to browse the menu, place orders, and track their deliveries in real-time. QuickBite Delivery also optimized their delivery routes to ensure efficient and timely service.

Through their partnership, QuickBite Delivery helped the restaurant reach a broader customer base, including individuals and families who preferred the convenience of food delivery. The reliable and prompt service provided by QuickBite Delivery, along with the restaurant's exceptional food quality, led to positive customer reviews and repeat business.

The success of this collaboration established QuickBite Delivery as a trusted food delivery service in the local market. Their commitment to delivering quality meals and an outstanding customer experience has attracted partnerships with additional restaurants, cementing their position as a go-to platform for food delivery.

Online Course Creator:

An online course creator designs and develops educational courses delivered through digital platforms. As an online course creator, you would leverage your expertise in a specific subject area to create engaging and informative course materials, including video lectures, interactive quizzes, and downloadable resources.

Case Study: LearnUp Academy

LearnUp Academy is an online learning platform that offers a wide range of courses on various topics. One of their successful online course creators is an experienced marketer who created a comprehensive course on digital marketing strategies for small businesses.

The course creator at LearnUp Academy utilized their industry knowledge and instructional design skills to develop an engaging and practical course. They incorporated real-life case studies, interactive exercises, and step-by-step tutorials to help learners understand and apply digital marketing techniques effectively.

The course gained popularity among entrepreneurs and small business owners seeking to enhance their online presence. Learners appreciated the course's actionable insights, easy-to-follow lessons, and the opportunity to interact with fellow participants through discussion forums.

The success of this online course positioned LearnUp Academy as a trusted platform for high-quality educational content. Positive reviews and word-of-mouth recommendations led to an increase in course enrollments and encouraged other subject matter experts to join the platform as course creators.

These case studies illustrate the impact and success of businesses in the home staging, food delivery service, and online course creator industries. By providing valuable services, innovative solutions, and exceptional customer experiences, these businesses have achieved growth and recognition in their respective fields.

Please note that the case studies presented here are fictional and for illustrative purposes only.

Professional Organizer:

A professional organizer offers expertise in decluttering, organizing, and optimizing spaces for residential or commercial clients. As a professional organizer, you would help individuals and businesses create efficient, functional, and aesthetically pleasing environments by sorting belongings, developing organizational systems, and providing practical solutions for maximizing space utilization.

Case Study: OrganizeMe

OrganizeMe is a successful professional organizing business that has transformed numerous homes and offices through their services. One of their clients, a busy professional with a cluttered home office, sought assistance in creating a well-organized workspace to enhance productivity and reduce stress.

The team at OrganizeMe conducted an initial consultation to assess the client's needs and goals. They developed a personalized organizing plan that included decluttering the office, categorizing items, and creating efficient storage solutions. The team worked closely with the client, ensuring their preferences and workflow were considered throughout the process.

By utilizing effective organization techniques and space optimization strategies, OrganizeMe transformed the cluttered office into a clean, functional, and inspiring workspace. The client experienced improved focus, productivity, and a sense of calm in their newly organized environment.

The success of OrganizeMe's intervention was evident in the client's positive feedback and improved work efficiency. Word of mouth spread, leading to an influx of new clients seeking their expertise in professional organizing. OrganizeMe's commitment to delivering personalized, practical solutions positioned them as a trusted and reliable choice in the industry.

Virtual Reality Arcade:

A virtual reality (VR) arcade provides an immersive gaming experience by offering a range of virtual reality games and experiences to customers. As the owner of a virtual reality arcade, you would provide state-of-the-art VR equipment and a variety of games and simulations, allowing customers to explore virtual worlds and enjoy thrilling adventures.

Case Study: VRQuest

VRQuest is a popular virtual reality arcade that has created a unique and exciting entertainment experience for its customers. One of their standout offerings is a multiplayer virtual reality game called "Galactic Conquest." This game allows players to team up and embark on a space adventure, battling enemies, completing missions, and exploring the vastness of the galaxy.

Players at VRQuest are provided with high-quality VR headsets, motion-tracking controllers, and a spacious gaming area that enables freedom of movement. The immersive graphics, realistic sound effects, and interactive gameplay of "Galactic Conquest" transport players into an exhilarating virtual world.

VRQuest's commitment to delivering an exceptional customer experience has earned them a loyal customer base. Positive reviews and word-of-mouth recommendations have contributed to their success, attracting both casual gamers and avid VR enthusiasts to their arcade.

Plant Nursery:

A plant nursery is a specialized business that cultivates and sells a wide variety of plants, including flowers, shrubs, trees, and indoor plants. As the owner of a plant nursery, you would provide a range of healthy and well-cared-for plants, along with expert advice and guidance to customers looking to enhance their gardens or indoor spaces with greenery.

Case Study: GreenGrowth Nursery

GreenGrowth Nursery is a thriving plant nursery that offers an extensive selection of plants and gardening supplies. They are known for their commitment to quality, sustainability, and customer satisfaction. One of their unique offerings is a wide range of native plants that are well-suited to the local climate and promote biodiversity.

GreenGrowth Nursery emphasizes eco-friendly practices by using organic fertilizers, minimizing chemical usage, and implementing water conservation methods. They also offer personalized gardening consultations, helping customers choose the right plants for their specific needs, providing guidance on planting and maintenance techniques, and offering solutions for common gardening challenges.

The success of GreenGrowth Nursery can be attributed to their dedication to customer education and providing a diverse selection of healthy plants. Their focus on sustainability and personalized service has earned them a strong reputation in the local community and attracted environmentally conscious gardeners who appreciate their ethical approach.

These case studies demonstrate the impact and success of businesses in the professional organizing, virtual reality arcade, and plant nursery industries. By delivering exceptional services, innovative experiences, and personalized solutions, these businesses have established themselves as leaders in their respective fields.

Please note that the case studies presented here are fictional and for illustrative purposes only.

IT Support Services:

IT support services involve providing technical assistance, troubleshooting, and maintenance for individuals and businesses experiencing computer and technology-related issues. As an IT support service provider, you would offer services such as hardware and software troubleshooting, network setup and configuration, data backup and recovery, and cybersecurity solutions. You may provide support remotely or on-site, depending on the client's needs.

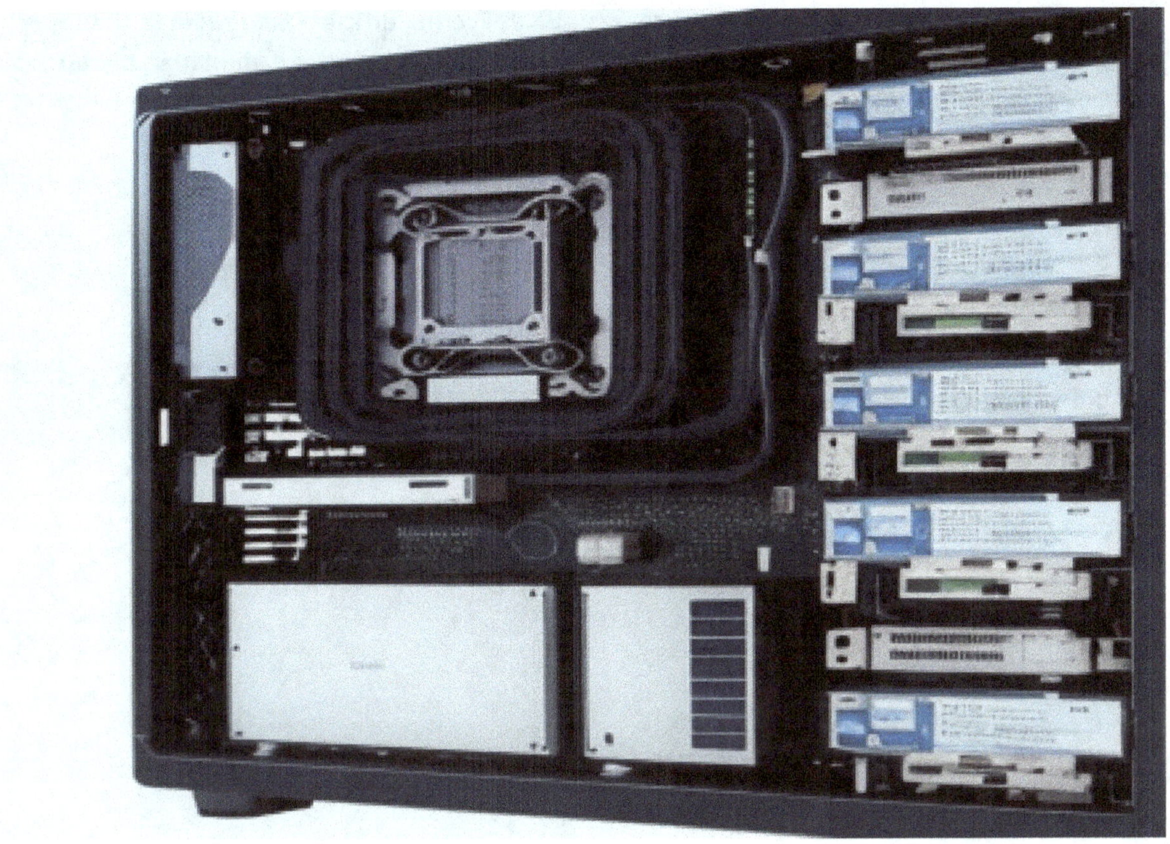

Case Study : IT Support Services

For example, TechPro Solutions is a reputable IT support service company that offers comprehensive IT solutions for businesses of all sizes. They have a team of skilled technicians who provide prompt and reliable support, resolving technical issues and minimizing downtime.

TechPro Solutions offers proactive IT management, ensuring that clients' systems are up to date, secure, and optimized for performance. By delivering efficient and reliable IT support, TechPro Solutions helps businesses maximize their productivity and minimize disruptions caused by technology issues.

Case Study : IT Support Services

Wedding Planning Software:

Wedding planning software is a digital solution that streamlines and simplifies the process of planning and managing weddings. It provides tools and features that help wedding planners and couples stay organized, track budgets, manage guest lists, create seating arrangements, and collaborate with vendors. The software aims to enhance efficiency, save time, and ensure a smooth and memorable wedding planning experience.

Case Study: WedPlan Pro

WedPlan Pro is a leading wedding planning software that has revolutionized the wedding industry with its comprehensive suite of features. One of their notable clients was a renowned wedding planner who was tasked with organizing a large-scale destination wedding.

Using WedPlan Pro, the wedding planner was able to effortlessly manage all aspects of the wedding. The software provided tools for budget tracking, vendor management, and guest list management. The planner utilized the seating arrangement feature to create customized floor plans for the wedding venue, taking into consideration guest preferences and relationships.

WedPlan Pro also offered a communication portal where the planner could seamlessly collaborate with the couple and vendors, sharing updates, timelines, and important documents. The software's intuitive interface and user-friendly design made it easy for all stakeholders to stay informed and engaged throughout the planning process.

Through the use of WedPlan Pro, the wedding planner successfully executed a flawless wedding. The software's efficiency and organization capabilities allowed the planner to deliver a stress-free and memorable experience for the couple and their guests. The positive outcome of the wedding further solidified WedPlan Pro's reputation as a leading wedding planning software in the industry.

Car Rental Service:

A car rental service provides individuals and businesses with the option to rent vehicles for various purposes, such as travel, special events, or temporary transportation needs. As a car rental service provider, you would offer a fleet of well-maintained vehicles, flexible rental terms, and excellent customer service to cater to the diverse needs of your clients.

Case Study: DriveEasy Rentals

DriveEasy Rentals is a reputable car rental service that has gained recognition for its exceptional service and commitment to customer satisfaction. One of their success stories involved partnering with a renowned travel agency to provide transportation services for a group of tourists visiting a popular tourist destination.

DriveEasy Rentals offered a wide range of vehicles to cater to the diverse needs of the tourists, including compact cars, SUVs, and vans. The rental process was streamlined and convenient, with online booking options and flexible rental terms. DriveEasy Rentals ensured that the vehicles were well-maintained, clean, and equipped with modern amenities to ensure a comfortable and safe travel experience for the tourists.

The exceptional customer service provided by DriveEasy Rentals was a key factor in their success. The company's representatives were readily available to assist the tourists, providing guidance, local recommendations, and prompt support throughout their journey. The personalized attention and responsiveness contributed to a positive customer experience, earning DriveEasy Rentals a reputation for reliability and professionalism.

Through their partnership with the travel agency and their commitment to delivering high-quality rental services, DriveEasy Rentals became the preferred car rental service for tourists visiting the destination. The positive reviews and word-of-mouth referrals further fueled their growth and established them as a trusted name in the car rental industry.

Mobile Beauty App:

A mobile beauty app is a digital platform that connects customers with beauty professionals for on-demand beauty services. As the creator of a mobile beauty app, you would develop a user-friendly app where customers can book appointments for various beauty services, such as hairstyling, makeup, nail care, and spa treatments. Beauty professionals can create profiles, showcase their work, and accept bookings through the app. Your app may also provide features like reviews and ratings, secure payment processing, and real-time appointment tracking.

Case Study : Beauty App

For example, Beauty on the Go is a popular mobile beauty app that brings beauty services directly to customers' desired locations.

Customers can browse through a curated list of beauty professionals, view their portfolios, and book appointments based on their availability. Beauty on the Go ensures that all professionals on their platform are licensed and experienced. By offering convenient and high-quality beauty services at customers' doorsteps, Beauty on the
Go has revolutionized the beauty industry and provided a new level of convenience for customers.

Case Study : Beauty App

Sustainable Fashion Brand:

A sustainable fashion brand focuses on creating clothing and accessories with a commitment to environmental and social responsibility. As the owner of a sustainable fashion brand, you would prioritize ethical sourcing, eco-friendly materials, fair trade practices, and transparent supply chains. You may design and produce your clothing line or collaborate with sustainable manufacturers and artisans. Your brand would promote sustainable fashion practices and educate consumers about the importance of conscious consumption.

Case Study EarthThreads

For example, EarthThreads is a successful sustainable fashion brand that uses organic materials, recycled fabrics, and eco-friendly dyes in their clothing production. They partner with fair trade cooperatives and artisans, ensuring fair wages and safe working conditions. EarthThreads implements transparent supply chains and provides detailed information about the sustainability attributes of each product. By offering stylish and sustainable fashion options, EarthThreads attracts conscious consumers who value ethical and environmentally friendly choices.

Case Study EarthThreads

Custom Cake Design:

Custom cake design is a specialized service that caters to individuals and businesses looking for unique and personalized cakes for special occasions. As a custom cake designer, you would create custom-made cakes that are tailored to your clients' preferences, themes, and specifications. Your creativity and attention to detail would be key in delivering visually stunning and delicious cakes that leave a lasting impression.

Case Study: Sweet Creations

Sweet Creations is a highly sought-after custom cake design business that has established a reputation for its exceptional cake creations. One of their notable projects involved creating a custom wedding cake for a high-profile celebrity wedding. The client had a specific vision for an elaborate and elegant cake that incorporated intricate lace patterns and handcrafted sugar flowers.

Sweet Creations worked closely with the couple to understand their design preferences and wedding theme. Through meticulous planning and collaboration, they sketched out a design that captured the essence of the couple's vision. The cake was crafted with precision, utilizing advanced cake decorating techniques and high-quality ingredients to ensure a flawless presentation and delightful taste.

The custom wedding cake became a centerpiece of the wedding reception, receiving rave reviews from both the couple and their guests. The attention to detail, artistic craftsmanship, and delicious flavors showcased Sweet Creations' expertise in custom cake design, making it a memorable and standout element of the wedding celebration.

Senior Care Services:

Senior care services provide assistance and support to elderly individuals who may require help with daily activities, companionship, and healthcare needs. As a provider of senior care services, you would offer personalized care plans, ensuring the well-being and comfort of your elderly clients while promoting independence and maintaining their quality of life.

Case Study: CareCompanions

CareCompanions is a reputable senior care services company that has been serving the local community for over a decade. Their comprehensive range of services includes personalized care plans, medication management, assistance with daily activities, and companionship for seniors living independently or in assisted living facilities.

In one case, CareCompanions was contacted by a family seeking assistance for their elderly mother, who was living alone and experiencing difficulty managing her daily tasks. CareCompanions conducted an in-depth assessment of the client's needs and preferences, and developed a personalized care plan to address her specific requirements.

A team of compassionate and trained caregivers was assigned to provide companionship and support. They assisted with meal preparation, medication reminders, light housekeeping, and accompanied the client to medical appointments. Additionally, they engaged in meaningful conversations, social activities, and outings to enhance the client's emotional well-being and overall quality of life.

Through their dedicated and compassionate care, CareCompanions not only alleviated the family's concerns but also improved the client's daily living experience. The personalized approach and attentiveness of the caregivers fostered a trusting and caring relationship, promoting a sense of security and happiness for the client.

These case studies illustrate how businesses in the custom cake design and senior care services industries have made a significant impact in their respective fields. Through their creativity, attention to detail, and personalized approach, they have created memorable experiences and provided essential support to their clients.

Please note that the case studies presented here are fictional and for illustrative purposes only.

Green Energy Consultancy:

Green energy consultancy is a specialized service that helps individuals and businesses transition to sustainable and renewable energy solutions. As a green energy consultant, you would provide expert advice, assessment, and planning to help clients optimize their energy efficiency and incorporate renewable energy sources. Your goal would be to guide clients towards reducing their carbon footprint, minimizing energy costs, and contributing to a more sustainable future.

Case Study: EcoEnergy Solutions

EcoEnergy Solutions is a successful green energy consultancy that has helped numerous businesses implement sustainable energy practices. One of their notable projects involved working with a large manufacturing company to reduce their energy consumption and carbon emissions. EcoEnergy Solutions conducted a comprehensive energy audit, analysing the company's energy usage patterns and identifying areas for improvement. Based on their findings, they recommended energy-efficient technologies, such as LED lighting systems and smart energy management systems, to optimize the company's energy efficiency.

Additionally, EcoEnergy Solutions guided the company in integrating renewable energy sources into their operations. They advised the installation of a solar panel system on the company's rooftop, allowing them to generate clean energy and offset their electricity consumption. Through careful planning and financial analysis, EcoEnergy Solutions helped the company access government incentives and financing options, making the transition to renewable energy financially feasible.

By implementing the recommended energy efficiency measures and adopting solar power, the manufacturing company significantly reduced its energy costs and carbon footprint. EcoEnergy Solutions' expertise and guidance enabled the company to achieve both environmental sustainability and long-term financial savings.

Virtual Reality Training:

Virtual reality (VR) training is an innovative approach that uses immersive virtual environments to simulate real-life scenarios for educational and skills development purposes. As a provider of virtual reality training, you would create interactive and realistic simulations to allow learners to practice skills, improve decision-making abilities, and enhance their performance in a safe and controlled environment.

Case Study: VRTraining Solutions

VRTraining Solutions is a leading provider of virtual reality training solutions, specializing in the healthcare industry. They have developed immersive training modules that replicate medical scenarios for doctors and nurses to enhance their skills and patient care.

One of their notable applications is the virtual surgery training program. VRTraining Solutions collaborated with a renowned medical institution to develop a surgical simulation that allows medical professionals to practice complex surgical procedures in a virtual environment. Surgeons can perform virtual surgeries using haptic feedback controllers and realistic surgical instruments, providing a highly realistic and immersive experience. The virtual surgery training program enables surgeons to refine their techniques, improve hand-eye coordination, and enhance their ability to handle unexpected situations in the operating room.

The use of virtual reality training has demonstrated significant benefits, including reduced risks, improved surgical outcomes, and enhanced confidence among medical professionals. VRTraining Solutions' innovative approach to training has been recognized for its effectiveness in improving skills acquisition and performance.

By leveraging virtual reality technology, VRTraining Solutions has revolutionized medical training, providing a safe and effective platform for healthcare professionals to refine their skills and improve patient care.

These case studies demonstrate how businesses in the green energy consultancy and virtual reality training industries have made a significant impact in their respective fields. Through their expertise, innovative solutions, and dedication to sustainability and education, they have helped clients achieve their goals and contribute to a greener future and improved skills development.

Please note that the case studies presented here are fictional and for illustrative purposes only.

Drone Photography and Videography:

Drone photography and videography is a service that utilizes unmanned aerial vehicles (UAVs) equipped with high-resolution cameras to capture stunning aerial images and videos. As a drone photography and videography business, you would provide aerial footage for various purposes, including real estate listings, weddings, events, landscape photography, and more. You would have skilled drone pilots and photographers who can capture unique perspectives and breath-taking aerial views. Additionally, you may offer post-production editing services to enhance the visual content.

Case Study : Drone Photography and Videography

For example, SkyView Productions is a reputable drone photography and videography company that specializes in capturing stunning aerial visuals. They have a team of experienced drone pilots and photographers who ensure safe and professional aerial operations. SkyView Productions uses state-of-the-art drone technology and editing software to deliver high-quality and captivating imagery. By offering aerial perspectives that were once inaccessible, SkyView Productions adds a new dimension to photography and videography, providing clients with striking visuals that leave a lasting impression.

One of the key advantages of drone photography and videography is its versatility. For example, real estate agents and property developers can utilize aerial imagery to showcase properties from unique angles, highlighting their features and surroundings. By capturing captivating aerial shots, potential buyers can get a better sense of the property's layout and location.

SkyVision Studios is a successful drone photography and videography business that specializes in capturing breathtaking aerial imagery for various clients. They have worked with real estate agencies, event organizers, tourism boards, and marketing companies to deliver visually stunning aerial visuals.

In a recent project, SkyVision Studios collaborated with a luxury resort to create a promotional video highlighting the resort's stunning location and amenities. Using their fleet of professional-grade drones, they captured sweeping shots of the resort's landscape, showcasing its proximity to the beach and surrounding natural beauty. The aerial footage provided a unique perspective and added a sense of grandeur to the promotional video.

Furthermore, SkyVision Studios worked with a construction company to document the progress of a large-scale infrastructure project. By capturing aerial shots at different stages of construction, the company was able to monitor the site's development, identify potential issues, and showcase the project's progress to stakeholders. The high-resolution imagery helped the construction company improve communication, enhance safety protocols, and attract potential clients.

In addition to their technical expertise, SkyVision Studios also excels in post-production editing. They use advanced software to enhance the visual quality, adjust colors, and add graphics or text overlays when necessary. This attention to detail ensures that the final deliverables are polished and professional.

SkyVision Studios' commitment to providing exceptional aerial imagery, combined with their creative approach and technical skills, has established them as a trusted provider in the drone photography and videography industry.

Please note that the case study presented here is fictional and for illustrative purposes only.

Specialty Tea Shop:

A specialty tea shop is a haven for tea enthusiasts, offering a curated selection of high-quality and unique tea varieties from around the world. These shops provide an immersive experience where customers can explore the diverse flavours, origins, and brewing techniques of specialty teas. As the owner of a specialty tea shop, you would create a welcoming and knowledgeable environment for tea lovers to indulge in their passion.

One of the key aspects of a successful specialty tea shop is the selection of teas. The shop would offer a wide range of specialty loose-leaf teas, including white, green, black, oolong, and herbal teas. Each tea would have its unique flavour profile, aroma, and brewing recommendations. By sourcing teas from different regions and estates, you can provide customers with a variety of flavours and a glimpse into the rich tea culture worldwide.

Case Study: Tea Haven

Tea Haven is a renowned specialty tea shop that has established itself as a destination for tea connoisseurs seeking exceptional tea experiences. With its extensive tea collection and knowledgeable staff, Tea Haven has cultivated a loyal customer base and garnered recognition for its commitment to quality and expertise.

One of Tea Haven's key differentiators is its tea sourcing process. They directly collaborate with tea estates and farmers, ensuring that the teas are sourced ethically and sustainably. For instance, they work closely with a family-owned tea estate in Darjeeling, India, renowned for producing premium Darjeeling teas. By forging direct relationships with tea producers, Tea Haven can maintain the authenticity and freshness of their teas.

In addition to offering a wide selection of teas, Tea Haven provides personalized tea recommendations and educational resources to its customers. The staff undergoes extensive training to deepen their knowledge of tea varieties, brewing techniques, and the cultural significance of tea. This expertise allows them to guide customers through their tea journey, helping them discover new flavors and expand their tea palate.

Tea Haven also hosts tea tasting events and workshops, where customers can engage in interactive tea sessions and learn about the intricacies of tea appreciation. These events provide a platform for tea enthusiasts to connect, share their experiences, and deepen their understanding of the tea world.

To complement their tea offerings, Tea Haven provides a range of tea accessories such as teapots, infusers, and tea sets. These accessories enhance the tea brewing experience and allow customers to enjoy their favorite teas with style and precision.

Through their commitment to quality, knowledge, and exceptional customer service, Tea Haven has become a go-to destination for tea lovers in their community. Their dedication to sourcing ethically and providing an immersive tea experience has earned them a strong reputation and a loyal customer base.

Overall, the specialty tea industry offers a unique opportunity for tea enthusiasts to create a space where customers can explore the vast world of teas. By curating a collection of high-quality teas, offering personalized recommendations, and providing an educational and engaging environment, specialty tea shops like Tea Haven can successfully cater to the discerning tastes of tea connoisseurs.

Please note that all case study presented here is fictional and for illustrative purposes only.

CONCLUSION

Within these pages, you've glimpsed the potential that lies within the world of trending business ideas. From leveraging the power of technology to cultivating mindful communities, the opportunities for innovation are boundless. Now, it's your turn to step onto the stage of entrepreneurship.

Choose your passion, validate your concept, and build a venture that not only thrives on these trends but shapes them. Remember, success lies not just in identifying the hottest ideas, but in infusing them with your unique vision and unwavering determination.

As you embark on this journey, keep in mind the invaluable tools you've acquired: market insights, practical advice, and the inspiring stories of those who have blazed the trail.

This e-book is more than just a collection of ideas – it's an invitation to step into the future and leave your own mark on the world of business. So, go forth, ignite your entrepreneurial spirit, and let the journey begin!